TOP 10 UNSOLVED MURDER MYSTERIES OF ALL TIMES

NISHI

Copyright © 2020 NISHI PANDEY

All rights reserved.

ISBN: **9798720611187**

INTRODUCTION

This book throws light on some of the most hyped unsolved murder mysteries of all times.

Although there are many murder mysteries, but here I have tried to cover some of the most mind boggling and famous murder mysteries of all times.

I have conducted appropriate research and tried to come up with an accurate presentation of what actually happened and what could probably be the cause of the murders or who may possibly be responsible for them.

The purpose of this book is to spread awareness. We do not endorse any of the theories mentioned in this book. We only try to bring to you the stories and facts that are available upon research.

The main purpose of this book is to educate our readers and intrigue their minds with some though provoking questions and make them wonder about the possible culprit behind these murder mysteries.

CONTENTS

1	Nicole Brown and Ron Goldman Murder Mystery	Pg.01
2	Bob Crane Murder Mystery	Pg.05
3	The West Mesa Bone Collector	Pg.08
4	The Long Island Serial Killer	Pg.12
5	Jon Benet Ramsey Murder Mystery	Pg.14
6	The Zodiac Killer	Pg.18
7	Tupac Shakur Murder Mystery	Pg.21
8	The Black Dahila Murder Mystery	Pg.24
9	Jack The Ripper	Pg.28
10	The Tylenol Poisoning	Pg.30

PREFACE

Hi! My name is Nishi and I am a full time writer and content creator. I am glad to bring to you the **fourth book** of our **Top 10 series**. I wanted to bring to my readers a bundle of exciting and short Books and this is how I came up with the idea of the Top 10 series.

I hope that my readers will enjoy and support this edition of the Top 10 series as well. If you like reading the content in our book, then I request you to kindly check out the other books in this series as well.

Over the coming months, I will bring to you many more interesting books with fantastic information.

I hope you will like reading this book.

Thank you very much for all the love and support.

Regards,

Nishi.

1. NICOLE BROWN AND RON GOLDMAN MURDER MYSTERY

O.J. Simpson's Ex-Wife, Man Found Slain

Nicole brown Simpson was a resident of Los Angeles California. She was found dead on June 12 1994 near her residence, along with her rumored boyfriend Ron Goldman.

Nicole was the ex-wife of former Professional football player OJ Simpson. Due to the tumultuous relationship she shared with OJ Simpson, the two had taken divorce and she started living alone.

On the evening of the fateful day, Nicole was stabbed many times along with her boyfriend while they were returning from a stroll. Her body was found that night lying in a pool of blood. Ron's body was also discovered nearby. Upon discovery of the bodies, police was informed and Autopsy was conducted on the bodies of Nicole and Ron in an attempt to determine the cause of their death. The results of the autopsy established that they were stabbed multiple times and their throats were slit. The wound on brown's neck was so deep that it had almost decapitated her.

OJ Simpson naturally became the prime accused due to his history of bad behavior with Nicole. On many occasions previously, he had physically abused her, stalked her, abused her and threatened her with dire circumstances even after their divorce.

OJ also had prior record of domestic violence against Nicole Brown and this had made him the natural suspect in this case. Also the evidences found at the scene of crime also pointed to the same fact.

The case immediately grabbed national headlines and gained a lot of media attention. High profile criminal investigation was launched and a trial was held but later the charges could not be proved and OJ Simpson was formerly acquitted of all charges.

The Nicole and Ron murder case is one of the most famous and high profile murder mysteries of our Times and a lot of attempts were made to find out the person responsible for committing this grisly crime. This case got a lot of attention and it was extensively covered on both electronic and print media. But no one came up with any lead.

The evidences of the crime scene pointed that OJ Simpson might have been involved with the murder. The evidences that point to the involvement of OJ Simpson are as follows:

i) His blood was found at the murder scene.
ii) Samples of blood and hair of Brown and Ron was found in Simpson's car

iii) One of OJ's gloves was found at Nichols house while the other one was found at his own house.

iv) Even the bloody shoe prints at the crime scene matched the shoe prints of the shoes owned by OJ Simpson.

But even after all these evidences; OJ could not be framed by the police.

OJ Simpson had assembled a team of expert defense lawyers that were considered to be a dream team. They were able to give the case an unwanted turn by claiming it as an act of racism and oppression by white police and investigation authorities. The team of lawyers claimed that the law enforcement officials were trying to wrongfully frame OJ Simpson.

In a much publicized hearing, OJ Simson was summoned for a judicial hearing. The questioning continued for 3 hours and the police presented their claims and evidences. But the smart lawyers were able to protect OJ from all the charges and in the end; none of the charges could be proved in the court. Due to the lack of evidence, OJ Simpson was acquitted of all charges. After being acquitted, OJ vowed to find the real killers but he never turned up with any leads.

Later, in a civilian trial invoked by the victim's family OJ was found responsible for committing violence against Nicole. He was charged with a case of battery and assault and was fined 33.5 million dollars. He has not even paid the total fine amount till now.

Later in the year 2007, Simpson was again arrested in Las Vegas for breaking into a hotel room and stealing a sports memorabilia. He was once again arrested in the year 2018 and he was found guilty of 12 charges including battery, robbery and kidnapping.

He was sentenced for 33 years and was released on 1st October 2017. But the true killer of Ron and Nicole has not yet been identified/proved or punished. This high profile case of our time gained a lot of media attention and publicity but it remains a mystery even to this day.

2. BOB CRANE

Bob crane was a famous TV star of the sixties. He became famous for his role in serials like Hogan's Heroes where he was one of the main leads and also did some guest appearances in other shows.

On June 29th 1978, he was found dead in his apartment. He had two deep wounds above his left ear with an electrical wire wrapped around his neck.
It was clear from the scene of the crime that he was murdered brutally with his Blood splattered all over, on the wall, curtain and even at the ceiling. His pillow was completely drenched in his blood. The scene of crime was absolutely horrific with the victim's blood everywhere.

The gory murder of the former star showed that he was probably spending time in Bad Company. He was married to his High School love Annie Terzian and fathered three children from her. But crane often misused his celebrity status to meet women, get intimate with them and collect their nude photos. Bob's son confirms this but he adds that his father was not involved in drugs or any other such issues.

His son states that Bob loved women and women also liked him for his handsome and flamboyant personality. He also said that one John Henry carpenter a video equipment sales person from Sony who happened to be a friend of Bob used to help him in his sexual pursuits.

It is also believed that Bob Crane and John Carpenter were involved also in the making of porn. Although Bob was a good man, he had committed some mistakes like collecting the nudes of the women; he spent time with, keeping them in his books and sometimes even showing them to other people. This would have certainly infuriated certain people.

Robert says that two days before his death, Bob called him and told him that he was looking forward to put things right. He said that he was going to divorce his current wife and wanted to lose people like John Carpenter who head followed him to Phoenix Arizona, where he had recently shifted. Bob wanted to start a new life and wanted to clear himself from all the mess he had got himself into. He also told his son that John Carpenter had become a problem for him and he wanted to get rid of him as soon as possible. However that never happened.

Robert believes that as his dad tried to pull away from John Carpenter, he couldn't handle the rejection and got enraged and probably killed Bob in a fit of anger. Even eyewitnesses account states that the night before the murder, there was an argument between John Carpenter and bob at a club.

Upon investigation the police found there was no sign of forced entry into Crain's apartment which made them believe that the person who killed Bob was someone known to him. Blood was everywhere and traces of blood were found on carpenter's rental car and on its passenger door.

Going by the history shared between Bob and John and the recent split made John Carpenter one of the biggest culprit. But as DNA testing and other advanced investigation techniques were not available at that time, the charge on John Carpenter could neither be created nor proved. The mystery of the murder of Bob crane remains mystery even after the passage of four decades.

3. WEST MESA BONE COLLECTOR (2009)

On a morning in February 2009, a local resident was walking with her dog in Albuquerque West Mesa area when she stumbled upon a horrible discovery.

She found a bone that resembled the femur bone of a human sticking out of the ground. She immediately informed the police and the police started digging to unearth the remains and start their investigation.

Upon digging, the police managed to unearth the remains of around 11 females out of which one was that of a girl. Albuquerque West Mesa area had witnessed atleast 19 cases of disappearances of girls and women between 2003 and 2006. Most of these women were Latina in origin and were mostly involved in the profession of sex.

Over the next one year, investigation authorities were able to identify the remains of 10 women and one girl. The girl was the only one who was not a sex worker. She was 15 year old Jamie Barela who was last seen in the area with her 27 year old cousin Evelyn Salazar. The remains of Evelyn were also found there. There was another 15 year old by the name of Syllania Edwards, who happened to be the only black girl whose remains were found at the site. The other women whose remains were unearthed from the site were:

Veronica Romero, aged 28 years.
Monica Candelaria, aged 22 years.
Victoria Chavez, aged 26 years.
Doreen Marquez, aged 24 years.
Virginia Cloven, aged 24 years.
Julie Nieto, aged 24 years.
Cinnamon Elks, aged 32 years.
Gina Michelle Valdez, aged 22 years and she also happened to be 4 months pregnant.

After the disappearances were reported, when they actually happened, investigations were launched but nothing was found. It was believed that these women were killed by an unknown serial killer who later got the name, 'the west Mesa Bone Collector'.

However, even now, the remains of eight other missing women has not been found and neither has the West Mesa Bone Collector been identified. Also the public reaction and involvement in this serial murder case was very cold as generally it is seen that society doesn't care much about prostitutes.

There was no lead found in this case however one person known as Lorenzo Montoya is considered to be the prime suspect. He lived near the burial site and was arrested in 1999 for attempting to strangled a prostitute, but was later killed in the year 2006 by the boyfriend of another prosecute whom Lawrence was trying to kill. Montoya had hired a prostitute named Sherick Hill, and after she came, he tied her up and tried to strangulate her. Hill's boyfriend was waiting outside the house and when Hill didn't come out of the house at the time, she said she would, her boyfriend entered the house and killed Montoya in self-defense.

Thankfully the West Mesa murders and disappearances stopped happening after the death of Lorenzo making the authorities believe that he may be the infamous West Mesa Bone Collector.

Another prime suspect in this case is another person called, Joseph Blea. He was blamed to be the killer by his wife and ex-wife.

As soon as the news of discovery of human remains of 11 women in West Mesa site spread, the police received a call from Joseph's ex-wife, April Gillen, who told the police that she thinks that her husband was the killer.

Joseph's current wife, Cheryl Blea also believed the same and what lead her to believe that was:
i. A large collection of jewelry found at their home and that pile of yellow metal certainly did not belong to her or her daughter.
ii. She also found a collection of women underwear found in a shed in the backyard of their house.

Joseph Blea was already infamous for his habit of stalking prostitutes and was on the watch list of law enforcement agencies. And when the police got to him for questioning, they also found electrical tapes and ropes lying in the back of his car, which he could have used to commit the murders.

However, the police could not prove the charges or nap the convict. Meanwhile, Joseph Blea is serving a 36-year jail term for raping a 13-year old girl.

There is a crushing lack of evidence in the West Mesa Bone Collector case. Bodies, when found were in a badly decomposed state and no physical sample or DNA samples could be recovered from them that could lead the investigation to any logical conclusion.

There was also no one who came up with a lead or anyone with an eyewitness account. The case remains unsolved till date.

4. LONG ISLAND SERIAL KILLER (2010 - ?)

Ever since the year 2010, around 10 to16 people have died or disappeared in the area of Long Island New York. Investigators believe that this is the act of a serial killer. They also believe that the killer maybe a single person or probably a group of people.

Of the people who have disappeared or died most of them were women sex workers. It had been nearly 10 years for the police searching for the dead and disappeared when recently they came across remains of 10 bodies on a stretch of beach on the south shore of Long Island. This immediately caught National headlines and the Killer earned the name 'Long island serial killer'.

It is not known as to how they died or who killed them but one account of a sex worker name Shannon Gilbert became particularly famous. She disappeared in the year 2010 when she was last spotted leaving a client's house on foot and not getting in the car that had brought her there.

The incident is described by one resident of Oak Beach, named Gus Coletti. On the fateful day Gus had woken up at around 5:00 a.m. in the morning and was going about his daily chores, when he heard a loud banging sound on his door. He peered through a window and saw a woman standing there. She was in a state of panic.

Gus let her inside and she immediately started pleading him for help. He asked her to relax and sit down and dialed 911 and started explaining the situation while the girl screamed from behind that they were going to kill her.

Gus asked the young woman to tell what had happened but she suddenly became cautious of him and ran out of the door that was still open. Gus who was still on line with 911 informed them what had just happened.

At the same time Gus could see a black SUV coming closer and it seemed like it was searching for the young women. As the SUV reached the house the driver inquired about the women to which Gus replied that he has already informed 911. To this the driver responded by saying that he shouldn't have done that and that she is going to get in a lot of trouble.
The young woman after running from Gus's house reached another house in the neighborhood and asked for help before again running off disappearing in the dark not to be found till date.

5. JON BENET RAMSEY (1996)

Jon Benet was a 6 year old beauty pageant. She used to live with her parents and her brother at their home in Boulder Colorado. She was kidnapped from her house with the kidnappers leaving a long 3 page ransom note on the stairs. However later that day the dead body of John Bennett was recovered from the basement of her own house. This is how the story unfolded:

On the day prior to the date of murder, the Ramseys went to bed at 9:00 p.m. and that is when John Bennett also went off to sleep.
One of the parents woke up at 5:00 a.m. in the morning to find that John Bennett was not present in her room. She also found a ransom letter lying at the stairs. The letter demanded a ransom of $118,000 and stated that the kidnappers would call between 8 to 10 a.m. to give the instructions about how to deliver the money.

The family informed the police and waited for the kidnappers to call. After the timeframe provided by the kidnappers passed, the police asked them to check the house for any details or letters that they may be missing.

Upon searching the house they found the body of John Bennett from the basement of the house. She was murdered and her body carried signs of sexual abuse. Now there are many weird elements attached with this story that we are going to discuss now.

The ransom letter in itself was written in a way that it gave the impression that it was written by an amateur with a purpose of confusing the police. The letter was 3-page long, an extremely long letter as far as ransom notes go. Secondly, the amount of ransom demanded was exactly $118,000 and not a rounded off sum. It coincided with the fact that John Ramsey had received an equal amount of money as Christmas Bonus 1 week back.

If this letter was written by the kidnapper, then he must be someone who knew John Ramsey and also new about the bonus he had got. Or if it was written by a family member then it was clearly done with an objective to deflect investigation around people who knew the Ramseys.

Weirder is the fact that the paper on which the ransom letter was written belonged to the house of Ramseys. It is absolutely impractical to think that a kidnapper would break into a house and then sit down there to write a three page long ransom letter.

These facts made many believe that Jon Benet was killed by her, own parents or someone from the family. But the charges could never be proved. However, there are many theories:

1. It could also have been a very badly arranged setup by John Ramsey. In the basement where the body of John Bennett was found, there was a broken window and a footprint on a suitcase lying near it. However, the footprint was not found on the fresh snow outside the window.

On examining the contents of the suitcase it was found that it contained a blanket that had stains of semen on it. And weirdest of it all, the semen was of another family member, John's eldest son from a previous marriage. He didn't live with them and the police could find sufficient proof that he was not in Boulder Colorado, at the time of the murder.

2. Another theory States that Jon Benet's brother Burke had accidentally killed her and then the entire family tried to cover up the story by creating another story around it.

But the body not only had signs of sexual abuse but also of physical abuse and strangulation. If she was killed by mistake then these marks should not be there on her body.

The police also think that it may be the result of an altercation between John and Burke where he lost control and did the heinous crime. However the culprit could not be named because of lack of evidence and mis-handling of the Crime scene by the police and family members.

3. Another twist in the tale comes in the form of a 54 year old man named Gary Olivia who was also a resident of Colorado and was a pedophile.

He had allegedly confessed to his crime in a letter he wrote to his formed classmate, Michael Vail in which he mentions how much he loved Jon Benet and how just by looking at her beautiful face and her divine body, he felt good within him.

In that letter, he also confesses that he had killed other kids too and that after finding Jon Benet, he realized that it was wrong to kill those kids. He goes on to mention that by accident, he let Jon Benet slip and crack her skull while he watched her die.

Gary Olivia was a listed sex offender who also happened to stay nearby Ramsey's home and even after Michael Vail informed the police about the letters and calls he had received from Olivia describing the murder, the Boulder Police admitted Olivia as a suspect in this case only as late as the year 2000. This happened when the police arrested him on some other charges and then they discovered a photo of Jon Benet and a poem he had written for her named, **'Ode to Jon Benet'**. A stun gun was also recovered from him which, the Police believes may have been used by Olivia to subdue his prey.

However, DNA testing results could establish no connection of Gary Olivia with the crime scene and the police lost interest in him.

6. ZODIAC KILLER

Slayer of hikers resembles the Zodiac killer, police say

Zodiac killer is the name given to another serial killer whose acts of murder haunted Northern California between late sixties and early seventies. As of now, the police have found evidence that he killed five people The Killer himself claims that he had killed 37 people over the years.

The zodiac killer became famous for his cryptic letters and declaration of murders he used to send to local newspapers used to call himself, 'Zodiac'. There are many accounts of murders and attempted murders committed by the zodiac killer where the victims testified that the man who attacked them looked the same as the sketches released by the police.

The zodiac killer regularly made fun of the police and media by sending those cryptic letters mocking them and saying that is not possible for the law enforcement agencies to catch him.

Criminal Investigators and Psychologists have tried to find out the possible motives behind these attacks and they came to the conclusion that the possible motives can be the following:

i. Obsession with Astrology:

His obsession with astrology is evident from the very name and the symbol he had chosen for the world to know him by.

Such obsession is also found in other serial killers where they use astrology to justify their killings in the form of offerings to another higher, other-worldly power.

His way of murders and the number of murders he would commit in each attempt, made it even clearer that he was deriving his methodology from astrology.

ii. Resentment towards Romantic Relationships:

This is another common reason for the weird behavior of some serial killers. Some people are just unable to handle rejection. If at any stage of life they face rejection from a girl, they get so badly hurt that their emotions of anger and self-pity starts fueling their dark side. This is how many killers are born.

The Zodiac's hatred towards couples shows a possible sexual inability that the convict faced or a feeling of rejection that had transformed into a feeling of hatred towards all romantic pairs.

This is also evident from the way he used to kill the pairs. Often the male victim received less wounds than the female victim. Like in the case of Betty Lou and David, where

Betty was shot 5 times while David was shot just once at 'point blank range'.

Some believe that the first kill of the Zodiac killer could have been the murder of an eighteen year old female college student in 1966. This girl might have been the original source of Zodiac's anger. Upon venting his anger out, he would have felt a kick like the one felt by first time drug addicts. This would have leaded him to kill more victims in search for reliving the moment.

iii. Superiority Complex:

This is another common motive found in many serial killers. People with such demented minds are often those who have lived a troubled life. It can be family issues, money related issues, and sexuality related issues or harassment by friends at school. All this develops a feeling of deep resentment inside a person, but he was not able to vent his feelings out on his true culprits or was just unable to do so. This gives rise to a dark personality that overtakes the sanity inside your mind.

It is believed that the Zodiac killer also likes a life where he was disrespected, not recognized and probably rejected. The killings made him feel more powerful. The torment of his victims and the control he exerted over them made him feel God like. The moments when he killed people were like his moments to rise and shine.

This feeling of control over his victims, the power to give life or death, compensated his life of mediocrity and filled him with a superiority complex..

7. MURDER MYSTERY OF TUPAC SHAKUR

RAP'S TUPAC DIES

Tupac Shakur received four shots to his chest at an intersection in Las Vegas. He was rushed to a hospital where he succumbed to his wounds, six days later on 13th September, 1996. The uncooperative list of witnesses and lethargic follow-up by Police, has left the case unsolved even after two decades.

All evidences point to the fact that the murder of Tupac Shakur was the result of a rivalry between east coast and west coast rappers and gang members.

It is believed that Tupac was a member of the gang named 'Mob Piru Bloods' and this gang were having a rivalry with the 'Southside Crips gang' from Crompton, California. The murder of Tupac Shakur was also a result of this rivalry.

Tupac had gone to see a Mike Tyson prize fight in Las Vegas. After the fight, as he exited from the venue, he bumped into a Southside Crips gang member and got involved in a fist fight with him. The name of the crips gang member was, Orlando Anderson.

It is believed that after getting thrashed at the hands of Tupac and his bodyguards, Orlando rushed back to his gang and asked them to help him take revenge and they complied.

It is also believed that Tupac's rival rapper Notorious B.I.G. (actual name: Christopher Wallace) was also involved in the killing. Infact he had declared a prize money of $1million for any crips gang member that would kill Tupac. It is supposed that the gun used for the killing was provided by Christopher Wallace.

That night, Tupac was in Las Vegas and was travelling in his friend's (Marion 'Suge' Knight) BMW and heading towards the hotel he was staying, when at a road intersection, a white cedilla came along and an unknown gunman fired many bullets on the BMW. Tupac sustained 4 bullet wounds and succumbed to his injuries six days later.

The murder was certainly a result of gang rivalry and without any doubt Tupac Shakur was not an angel and he was not keeping good company either. But who was the one guy who actually fired on Tupac is still not proved.

However, 22 years later, the death-bed confession from a west coast gang member could help solve the murder mystery. Rapper Keffe D, also known as Duane Keith Davis on his death bed claimed that he knew what happened that night and who fired at Tupac. He disclosed this because he was suffering from cancer and his illness gave him immunity from prosecution.

He said that he was sitting in the front seat of the white Cadillac from which bullets were fired at Tupac. The car was being driven by Terrence Brown while Dre Smith and Orlando Anderson were sitting at the back seat. They all were members of the Crips gang and at the time of Keffe's confession, all Brown, Smith and Anderson were already dead.

He said that after Tupac's scuffle with Orlando Anderson, all these Cripps gang members were searching for Tupac and they eventually found him in that car. Upon being asked as to who exactly shot at Tupac, Keffe said that he would not tell that to uphold the 'Code of the Streets'. However, he did say that the shots came from the back seat of the car.

Police believes that it was Orlando Anderson, but he had already denied the charges earlier and now he was already dead so it was too late to take any action against him.

8. THE BLACK DAHLIA MURDER MYSTERY (1947)

GIRL TORTURED AND SLAIN
Hacked Nude Body Found in L. A. Lot

The murder of Elizabeth Short is one of the most gruesome unsolved murder mysteries in the history of Hollywood. Even after more than 7 decades of the heinous crime there is no clue of the culprit. Elizabeth short was an aspiring Hollywood actress who used to live in Los Angeles. In the year 1947 she was founded dead with her body lying on grass on the side of a road by a woman who had gone out to take a stroll with her daughter. Not only was Elizabeth shot dead but her body was brutally dismembered. Her body carried the marks of physical abuse and her body was completely dissected from Waste and her mouth was slashed from ear to ear giving it the notorious 'Glasgow Smile' expression.

There was no blood found at the scene of the crime pointing to the fact that she was killed somewhere else, there the killer had dissected her body and allowed all the blood to drain away and then brought and dumped the body there.

The body was so brutally dismembered and disfigured that it was difficult to ascertain the identity of the body. The police were able to identify that it was the body of

Elizabeth short only after they ran a scan on her fingerprints.

Elizabeth Short got the name of black Dahlia by people after her death when her murder resembled the story of the movie 'Blue Dahlia' that was released 1 year back. Although it was never ascertained as to who killed her and why, people have come up with many theories to explain the murder and guess who the killer actually was. Some of the theories are as under:

1. Cleveland Torso Murders: some linked the murder of Elizabeth Short with the Cleveland torso murders. as the way she was murdered resembled a lot to the way another serial killer in Cleveland killed people between 1934 and 1938. He claimed the lives of 12 victims and brutally dismembered their bodies after killing them.

One month after Elizabeth's murder, another woman's body was discovered in Los Angeles and the condition in which the body was found, resembled a lot like that of Elizabeth Short.

This body was also naked and lying in the grass. Her face was badly beaten up and on her stomach it was written f*** you BD.

People and investigators were quick to associate BD with the name Black Dahlia. Was this a clue? Was this lady murdered by the same killer, who killed Elizabeth Short? There are many unanswered questions that have not yet been answered. Who killed Black Dahlia remains a mystery to this day.

Overtime many people came to the forefront claiming that they did the murder. They did this to get some cheap publicity and the police was able to rule out all of them. The investigation agencies were however able to confirm that the killer was from a medical background due to the precision cuts he had made on the body. The dissection of the body was also done with the precision of a surgeon.

One story narrated by former LAPD detective Steve Hodel, however gained all attention. His father, Dr.George Hodel had left the family early on but he connected with his son Steve in his last days.

After George's death, Steve was going through his belongings once and he found a photo frame with the photo of a lady that looked exactly like the Black Dahila. Steve was shocked to find this and decided to investigate the relations of his father with Elizabeth Short and find out if he was the one responsible for her murder.

Upon conversation with his half-sister Tamara Hodel, he came to know that their father was a suspect in Black Dahila murder case. Upon knowing this, Steve became more determined to prove that his father had nothing to do with the murder. He set out to know more about his father's connection with Elizabeth Short in an attempt to exonerate him.

George had connections with groups involved in sex and drugs and so he was put under surveillance by the L.A.P.D. In one of the recordings George could be heard saying, **"Supposing' I did kill the Black Dahlia. They couldn't prove it now. They can't talk to my secretary anymore because she's dead."**

In another such horrific recording, he could be heard saying **"Maybe I did kill my secretary."** And while he was saying so, a woman's scream could be heard in the background. It made Steve believe, that George may have killed both Elizabeth and his secretary who probably knew about what George had done.

There were some other evidences, Steve could find against his father. In one such evidence, George found two 1930's photos taken by Man Ray who was a surreal photographer and a friend of George. The photos resembled the pose in which Elizabeth's body was found lying in the grass. Steve argues that George may have used the murder to emulate the art of Man Ray.

Steve also says that he has found connection of his father with many other cases of murders in Los Angeles around the same time. He says that the police at that time had a pretty clear case against George but were unable to nab him.

Without any official statement about the murderer and the murder mystery, the case remains unsolved even to this day.

9. JACK THE RIPPER

Jack the Ripper was one of the earliest serial killers whose acts of murder inspired many movies, works of literature and also a whole new generation of serial killers that kept popping with an increased frequency after him.

He was a killer who terrorized Britain between 1888 and 1892. He was speculated to have committed over a dozen murders but five cases of murders were attributed to him with proof. All of his victims were women and were engaged in the profession of prostitution.

He was known for dismembering his victim's body and his modus operandi indicated that he had good knowledge of human anatomy as in one case of murder, he had mailed half-a-kidney of his victim to the police.

The identity of Jack the Ripper remains unknown even to this date. However, there were a few suspects namely:

i) Montague Druitt who was a barrister and a teacher with some background in surgeries.

ii) Michael Ostrog, who was a Russian criminal and physician.

iii) Aaron Kosminski who was a Polish immigrant living in Whitechapel area.

Jack the Ripper committed atleast 5 murders that are associated with him near the Whitechapel area. The murders came to be known as the 'Whitechapel Murders'.

Jack was never identified. He had managed to spread widespread panic among the people of Britain and the Police department drew a lot of criticism for their inability to nab the killer resulting in the loss of innocent lives.

10. THE TYLENOL POISONINGS (1982)

In the year 1982, seven people died in Chicago after consuming Tylenol pills laced with cyanide. This filled the people with fear and hysteria and everyone was scared before taking a medicine.

Today, we consume medicines without any worry or fear, expecting them to help us recuperate. But imagine if the pills we often consumed were laced with a deadly poison that can take our lives.

A similar horrific incident took place in the year 1982 when someone managed to lace the Tylenol tablets with cyanide. People consumed Tylenol as a pain reliever, but little did they know that this simple pain reliever had been turned into a lethal dose of death.

After the deaths, there was a huge uproar, but the parent company 'Johnson & Johnson' was able to hush up the entire incident and came out of the issue unscathed and eventually regain the lost trust.

But it was never found or revealed as to who was the person responsible for lacing the Tylenol tablets with cyanide and the case remains a mystery even to this day.

CONCLUSION

These were some of the most intriguing murder mysteries of our times. While some of them have an obvious suspect, the others are totally a dark mystery.

Mankind is capable of doing both good and bad. While generally people like to live a life of good, there are some who are more inclined towards their dark side.

Over the course of human history, many murderers and serial killers have reared their ugly head and scarred humanity forever. It is therefore important to stay aware of our surroundings and the people living around us.

It is important to stay vigilant at all times because we may never know when the devil will strike.

****
****
****

Printed in Great Britain
by Amazon

33777106R00030